12^{50} MD

THE AMAZON'S HERO

BOOKS BY THE SAME AUTHOR

Demon in Love
The Early Land
The Flying Ones
The Magic Child
Three Loves the Same
Some Phoenix Blood
Flower Myth

THE AMAZON'S HERO

A TWO-ACT PLAY IN VERSE

By

HORATIO COLONY

Boston
BRANDEN PRESS
Publishers

Standard Book Number 8283-1340-7
© Copyright, 1972, by Branden Press
Printed in the United States of America
Library of Congress Catalog Card Number 73-182864

THE AMAZON'S HERO

The characters are HIPPOLYTA, *queen of the Amazons,* ANTIOPE, *her lieutenant and confidante,* HERCULES, *the Greek hero,* and other Amazons.

The scene is in a wood in the heart of the Amazon kingdom.

ACT I

Curtain rises on an open place in the middle of the thick woods. The Amazons enter with Hippolyta *and* Antiope. *Enter a messenger.*

Messenger

Where is Hippolyta? I must see her.

Hippolyta

Stop here and give your message, nice young man.

Messenger

There is a man coming here, one Hercules,
To get the dear queen's girdle.

Hippolyta
     For himself?

Messenger

No, for some princess.

Hippolyta
     What, in the very heart
Of my kingdom? Where indeed are all my guards?
Women, come round and do your soldiering.

Messenger

But this man's bigger than a common man.

Hippolyta

Lay here the ambush; then I will confront him
Alone. You follow. We will peek at him.
    (All go out. Enter Hercules.*)*

HERCULES
This is the place. The warlike women live
Not far away from here. Hey, what is this?—
The tracks of women. Now my heart comes red.

(Enter HIPPOLYTA.)
HIPPOLYTA
Who are you? Why do you come to this land?

HERCULES
I'm Hercules. What are you—a stout fellow
Or a soldier boy? But tell me, where's your beard?
You should boast at least two hairs upon your lip.

HIPPOLYTA
I'm the queen of all this young, brave woman-land.

HERCULES
Well, whatever you are, come here, companion me.
I'm known as a comrade. Walk along with me,
And near some brook we'll come to a short halt
To swim in it. Have you something sweet and coarse
For an adventuring one, a down-and-out?

HIPPOLYTA
Come, insolent, advance not one more step
Or down you go.

HERCULES
                    But all the men go down
Before me also. I am Hercules.
Have you not heard? All men turn into girls
Or pools of soft cow's milk when I look straight
At them. But tell me, what's that thing you wear?

HIPPOLYTA
A girdle. And you know it very well.

HERCULES
I want that girdle. I must have that girdle.
The princess Admeta wants that bully belt.
The gods alone know why she wants your belt.
Perhaps you know.

HIPPOLYTA
                Then you, a wonderman,
Take orders from a woman?

HERCULES
                Yes, I do.—
The gods decree it.

                (He takes hold of the girdle.)

HIPPOLYTA
                Stand back, you man.
Know you that man's big feet have no place here.
This is woman's earth.

HERCULES
                Enough. I hear you, woman.
This earth belongs to me. Each stream is mine
To drink or bathe in. Every barn is mine
To sleep in, every forest mine to hunt in.
Women are mine, and girls and boys and men.
Horses are mine—

HIPPOLYTA
                Ah, insolent enough.
And shall I strike you?

HERCULES
                    Then you will be struck.
Think not because you are a woman you
Can say and not be made to hurt for it.
I am no woman-lover, Venus-lover.
Women are bitches, heifers, and brood mares
Or even less. And with my own good foot
I handle them. My grievous greedy feet
Have pushed a goodly number from my bed.

HIPPOLYTA
Another word and I will strike you down.

HERCULES
Come, do it, queen. Come on, close bellies with me.
Crotch and uncrotch me, but I'll have your girdle.
The princess Admeta has sent me for it—
She, too, a woman, but the gods ordain it—
Not she.

HIPPOLYTA
Hands off my girdle. Do not touch it.

HERCULES
I must have it. Why, it's only a deer's rawness.
Give me the girdle. See, my hand's already
Between it and your flesh. One little pull
And off it comes. My foot is on your foot.
My big toe conquers you.

HIPPOLYTA
              Let go, you oaf.
You beast, you rough of neck.

HERCULES
>Here, take my club
In fair exchange, and also my leather belt.
Come, give it me, you pretty queen of bitches
You whore without men.
>*(He starts to pull off the girdle.)*

HIPPOLYTA
>Come, girls; come, women!
Seize him who would rape off the royal belt,
Taking it from me.
>*(They rush at him.)*

HERCULES
>Why, here are all the whores
Of Caucasus. Girls, go and get stiff drunk.
Nor can you make me drunk with your soft blows,
But I can drunken you. Why such a mill
And jab of hands is but a flow of water
Down my back.
>*(He flings the Amazons about.)*

HIPPOLYTA
>Antiope, lead on the girls.

ANTIOPE
Highness, I do the very best I can,
But you see his strength, the hammer of his anger.

HIPPOLYTA
Get down beneath him, get on top of him.
Battle and bruise him.
>**(HERCULES** *throws them down.)*

HERCULES
                    See, O valiant queen,
How your women-warriors fall away from me.
Come, watch your head as I make a down dive
At your left foot. Your heel I'll hold up high
As though it were an apple; and I'll make
Light of your backsides.
                    (He throws the queen down.)
                    Get up again, my love.
Would you prefer to fall down from an Arm Drag
Or from an arm Grape-Vine? Or what would you?
Now let's see you break out of the Cross Buttock.
You know as much of buttocks and of balls
As any woman.

(He throws the queen again. The Amazons rush in.)

HIPPOLYTA
                    Hold, don't hurt the man.
For once a man lies not about his strength.
I would not see him harmed. He only wants
My belt.

HERCULES
                    That's all, and I will leave your land.

HIPPOLYTA
You'll have it then, but first stay here with us.
Enjoy our life, for we are both the same
Beneath the skin, and yet you are a male
And I am something better.

HERCULES
                    Good girls and all,
I need not hurry off with the good girdle.
You girls are as good comrades as the men,

[12]

And lazy, too, and just as invitatious.
Pour out for me your rustic sour wine
And give me meat. I also see you ladies
Are not afraid to spit or very much scared
Of sweaty fragrance.

     HIPPOLYTA
       Do not guy my girls.

     HERCULES
No, I admire them more than I can tell.
I like your bodies and your polished pieces,
Your fine stout horses. Yet though I admire
I kill for treachery, so do not meddle
With my sleep or dreams. I go into this cave.
Beware, my dears, beware.

     HIPPOLYTA
      Rest you in peace.

        (He goes out.)

     ANTIOPE
You will not let him wake. I tell you kill him.
Did he not dare to throw you?

     HIPPOLYTA
      Yes, he did.
And I love him for it.

     ANTIOPE
      Then you will not kill him?

     HIPPOLYTA
No, I won't.

ANTIOPE
					He will scoff at you and us.
This princess-girl also will point her finger
Of scorn at us for giving up our clothes.

HIPPOLYTA
I don't care what they say.

ALL
					You mustn't lose face.

HIPPOLYTA
I don't want shedding blood.

ALL
					Since when have you
Feared to shed blood.

HIPPOLYTA
					I like to shed the blood
Of our enemies; but this great, handsome fellow
Cannot be called our hater.

ALL
					You should kill him.
You must, Hippolyta, you must, you must,
Or you can never more be queen of us.

(They crowd around her.)

HIPPOLYTA
Don't touch me, girls. Don't dare to touch me.

ALL
As yet we warriors have not slain a queen,
But men have. We can be like them in that.

[14]

HIPPOLYTA

What, dare you threaten. Dare you to lay hand
On me, your queen?

ALL
We made you. We'll unmake you.

HIPPOLYTA

Antiope, are you for them or me?

ANTIOPE

I'm for them. You must not give away the belt.

HIPPOLYTA

Step back there, women.

(Enter HERCULES.)

HERCULES
What ho, what's all this?
Get back there, touch her not. I can slay women
As readily as men.
(He drives them back.)

HIPPOLYTA
They mean no wrong.
I'll go and bring them back. Wait here awhile.
They do not wish me to give up the girdle.

HERCULES

Why then I'll mow them down.

HIPPOLYTA
Don't do it yet.

Be different for a change.

HERCULES
How, how so?

HIPPOLYTA
Couldn't you steal it? Couldn't we have a revel?
The Amazons like all good soldier men
Are fond of liquor; we could get them drunk.
You could take my girdle then, or we could lose it
In a betting game. Now to be frank with you
My sisters often are in a quandary
With hating men and wishing to be like them.

HERCULES
Then you have this same wish?

HIPPOLYTA
I have my days
Of woman, but I hide it from my soldiers.

HERCULES
If that is so, O queen, I cannot wait
For night to hug you to my handsome breast
In my strong arms.

HIPPOLYTA
Oh, so you think you're handsome?

HERCULES
I do; and since I think it why not say so.

HIPPOLYTA
Why not, indeed, my friend? But there are some
Who'll say you are not handsome, with your face
And eyes too round, your short hair twisted tight,
Your neck too short, your forearms much too large.

HERCULES
I care not for them; I am Hercules
And think myself most handsome with my face
And body shaped by the green death of snakes
And the lion-death. Behold me, little one.

HIPPOLYTA
I like you, sir, the more you talk to me.

HERCULES
Behold me.

HIPPOLYTA
     I could fall in love with you.

HERCULES
There are a thousand reasons for so falling
And a thousand for not falling.

HIPPOLYTA
     But very soon
I'll cease to reason.

HERCULES
     Are you that far gone?

HIPPOLYTA
Almost; I love you truly.

HERCULES
     No, you don't.
There's always the untrueness.

HIPPOLYTA
     Well, I love you
As much as flesh can.

[17]

HERCULES

How do you feel now?
Do I raise the woman in you or the man
Or both together? Are you boy or girl?

HIPPOLYTA

You raise the girl in me.

HERCULES

Indeed, who cares
What rises up in one; the good thing is
What rises up on one.

HIPPOLYTA

I do adore you.
I am all woman; never was I queen.
I have no business here to rule these women.
I never had a talent for that rule
And only thought so; water is not weaker
Than I; and all this reasoning on love
Has but caught my foot in traps; this great Eros
Has his revenges.

HERCULES

Come, bear up, my girl.

HIPPOLYTA

I know you love me not; and that you would
Take advantage of me.

HERCULES

It's what I intend;
I'll reap you with robustness, without taint
Of love.

[18]

HIPPOLYTA
              And knowing you care not for me,
I'll fling myself into your arms.

HERCULES
              Why not?

HIPPOLYTA
Think of all I give.

HERCULES
              Now you are bartering.

HIPPOLYTA
Oh, please don't mock at me; I do adore you.
I give all this to you, this land of grapes,
So goodly with its vines.

HERCULES
              You throw it all
Away?

HIPPOLYTA
Yes, gladly.

HERCULES
              O you silly fool.

HIPPOLYTA
Did you not cast your strength out the window
For other girls?

HERCULES
              It is too far much mine
To cast away. I know it far too well.

HIPPOLYTA
How can you love me when you talk so much?
I love; and Eros has smitten me with talk—
Love can make speechless, another one he fills
Up to the lips with words.

HERCULES
                And now you reason.

HIPPOLYTA
O heavens no, but come and stay with us
And be our king. I care no more for rank.
I would rather be a woman of the people
Than queen.

HERCULES
         You think so now, but later, later?

HIPPOLYTA
Later is later. Now is powerful now.

HERCULES
You never could do without your rank, my love.

HIPPOLYTA
No, I want to shame myself before my people.
I'll give you the belt.

HERCULES
               Shush, not so fast, my love.
Hear me as I whisper. We must plan it.
I'll pretend to steal the girdle, but all this
Will happen later.

Hippolyta
                    Yes, let's go away.
Take me away. You can abandon me
When you wish; but no, do not abandon me.

Hercules
You gracious fool, why, you're adorable.

Hippolyta
I love to have you say so.

Hercules
                    Come and kiss
With me.
                            (Antiope *comes in.*)
Antiope
                    She shall not go away with you.

Hippolyta
How dare you say it. Get out of my path,
You woman.

Antiope
            Shame on you, Hippolyta.

Hippolyta
I want to be more shameful.

Antiope
                        If you leave
Our people with this man, you are no longer
The queen.

Hippolyta
            Then you'll be queen instead of me.

[21]

ANTIOPE

Well, I may have to be.

HIPPOLYTA

You make me laugh.

ANTIOPE

I'll be the last to laugh.

HERCULES

Oh, this is good.
I love to see bulls, goats, and crickets fight.
Dogs are the best, but next to dogs are women.

HIPPOLYTA

Oh, let her talk. I don't care what she says.
I wish no longer to be queen of all
These manly bitches. I would rather be
A housewife in the meanest household with
The man of my desire. Antiope, you can
Be queen for me; I give all power to you.
Act queen to heart's content; I wish you well.

ANTIOPE

Do you mean it?

HIPPOLYTA

Yes, I do.

ANTIOPE

Well, I'll not be it
From your hand; I will depose you.

HIPPOLYTA

Call it that,
If you wish it.

[22]

ANTIOPE
> Ho, all Amazons, I'm queen.
You must obey me now; Hippolyta
Has become a woman.

HIPPOLYTA
> Do you think I care?
Let her have the queenship, with the good and bad—

HERCULES
But you'll regret this later; so you must
Keep your queenship.

HIPPOLYTA
> It is nothing to me now.

HERCULES
You must not give it up; look here, you girl,
You're not the queen as long as I am here—
And girls, the pack of you, each whore of you,
Your queen is still Hippolyta the famed;
Let not the least or greatest among you
Forget it, or show any lack of what
Is due a queen.

HIPPOLYTA
> Come, let us leave this, love.
Since you desire it, love, I shall stay queen.

HERCULES
I do desire it.

HIPPOLYTA
> Take me from this place.

HERCULES
Let's camp here, have our love nest on this spot.
I'll chase the girls away.

HIPPOLYTA
No, we will go
Over there.

HERCULES
You know the good warm spots of earth.

HIPPOLYTA
I do, but come. I am so anxious now
To lead you somewhere.

HERCULES
Then come, lead me on.

HIPPOLYTA
Come, love.

(She leads him off.)

CURTAIN

ACT II

Same as first scene. Enter HERCULES *and* HIPPOLYTA.

HIPPOLYTA
You cannot leave here yet; you cannot, love.

HERCULES
But you said you'd go with me.

HIPPOLYTA
But these last days
Have been so good.

HERCULES
I'll say you have adored me—

HIPPOLYTA
You love me not, which makes me love you more.
The will-to-love makes me try all the more
To make you love; and yet there's bitter sweetness
In the lack of my success.

HERCULES
I love you truly.

HIPPOLYTA
You do not; little as I know of love,
I know your heart is just the apple it was
When you came here with the fool's pranks of you,
And your big prick.

HERCULES
You do not love me then?

HIPPOLYTA
What do you do? You run and skip a stone
On the water or you swing upon a tree,
Pulling its top down. You reach in a hollow
Of a tree to catch the bear by his short hair,
And laugh like mad.

HERCULES
                Why sure I do those things.
But now I want a rub down and some meat.

HIPPOLYTA
I'll get you a haunch of deer. I'll bring it in
Over my shoulder, and I'll quarter it
To your liking.

HERCULES
              Yes, but first drive off these flies.

HIPPOLYTA
I will, my love.

HERCULES
               And look you to my feet.
Rub my head now, and get a boxwood comb
And comb my hair. I swear I'm doing you favors
In letting you have play with my person—
Rump, ribs or round or else a piece of chine,
Haunch, leg, or breast. Or would you have my tongue
With its big roots, or even the cheeks of me.

HIPPOLYTA
My lovely one, and aren't you sleepy yet?

Hercules
No, you're my pillow. Get beneath my head.
You are all things to powerful Hercules.
You sweeten my life.

Hippolyta
Yes, I hope I do.

Hercules
Do you love me as much as ever you did?
I like to be kissed, and your lips cover me
All over.

Hippolyta
I and my mouth are small.

Hercules
Don't grow too big. Great men like little girls.

Hippolyta
But not as small as I have late become.
I am small beside Antiope, the others.
Above whom I was once the largest, strongest.
My love has made me little, taken all
Of the old force; but still the flowered path
Downward has joy which is not happiness.
I am joyous at my lessening all over,
While fearing that I may become so small
You cannot love me more.

Hercules
Come, my dear queen,
And be yourself again; you are no whit
Smaller than before; no, you are bigger.
Your mouth is larger and your eyes are larger;
And fortunate you are if you become
Not larger still.

HIPPOLYTA
But if you love me much
Why don't you ever grow small; I swear you are
Larger than when you came into our crowd,
Well traipsed with dust, and many little cuts
And wounds about the forearms and the knees.

HERCULES
That's enough. Let's go to sleep.

HIPPOLYTA
Oh yes, my dear.
Shall I watch, keep guard?

HERCULES
No need for that, my love.

HIPPOLYTA
But I shall watch.

HERCULES
Then watch for all I care.
Lay twigs around so that I can have fire
On waking up.
(He sleeps.)

HIPPOLYTA
Oh, he's a wondrous fellow.
Though I've given away my treasure and my power
I hold it cheap. Yet still I am the queen
While he stays here, but after he is gone
They will depose me for the glorious lapse
From the reason of our rule. My girdle gone,
I'll be no one. But here's Antiope.
(Enter ANTIOPE.)
What are you doing here? I thought we were
At odds?

[28]

ANTIOPE
      I would presume to be, my dear,
But in your own behalf, my dearest dear.

HIPPOLYTA
Then it was only ruse.

ANTIOPE
              Indeed it was.
You know we none of us are strong enough
To battle you; you also wear a wisdom
In your crown.

HIPPOLYTA
              No wisdom have I there,
For I'm in love; but still on certain mornings
I would I were not so.

ANTIOPE
              Fie, you were never
In love; it never once became your soul—

HIPPOLYTA
There are indeed times when I tire of this.

ANTIOPE
There will be more times still.

HIPPOLYTA
              Oh, I trust so.

ANTIOPE
You are too kind with him; he loves you too.

HIPPOLYTA
Oh, I think not.

ANTIOPE
I'd love to see you force him
To work for you as he did for Omphale.

HIPPOLYTA
I would not love him then.

ANTIOPE
Oh, you will force him.

HIPPOLYTA
Do you think so?

ANTIOPE
I know so.

HIPPOLYTA
Enough, enough.
He wakes up; go away.

ANTIOPE
But tell me first
Will you give up your girdle?

HIPPOLYTA
Never, never.
I'll die for it, I swear.

ANTIOPE
Good, my lovely queen.
Good, good.

HIPPOLYTA
Oh, please now, go away, my friend.

(ANTIOPE *goes out.*)

What she says is true; new moments come to me
When I am out of love; and back there comes
Into my heart a regal wishfulness.
O love, indeed, is wonderful enough,
But thrones are even more wondrous, and sweet power
Makes the very bones run honey. Can a person
Have two such sweetnesses, both love and power,
Or does one ruin but the other pleasure;
Which one lasts longer—love, sure, lasts the less—
It wounds that very one whose star is power;
If love's my star, why that's another thing—
I live by it; but if one breathes by power
Love's but a hurt; shall I go hurting me—
Making myself a fool-heart among women,
Or worse.

(HERCULES awakes.)

My friend, I'd like to speak with you.
Go away from here quick, quick before love dies.
Get on your feet and walk, get out of here.
I'll give you the girdle; you have no excuse
For longer staying here, take the girdle quick
And go.

HERCULES
Why should I, dear; I had a dream
Of you; I dreamt that I was mad for you—
So why should I not love you when awake.
Why should I not remain here in the woods
With you, forget my quests, stay here forever.
Why should I roam, why should I force this belt
Away from you; no keep it, keep it, love.

HIPPOLYTA
Please go. Please go.

HERCULES
    Oh, go get me a drink.

HIPPOLYTA
I beg you go; no good can come of this;
If you stay longer it will be the death
Of one of us or both.

HERCULES
    Ho, not of me.

HIPPOLYTA
Then of me.

HERCULES
    I don't believe it; I'll not go.
I'll stay right here, and you shall die your death
Of love.

HIPPOLYTA
    I fear.

HERCULES
    Fear not, but bring me water.

(She goes out.)

My faith, that is a woman for our taste
And beautiful; she puts my other girls
In the shade; by heavens but this woman suits me.
She has a way, she has a rosy neck;
I love her now; in faith, I love her much.
Tell me, does love come first or lying first;
I love when I lie and lie down where I love.
But she's a rare one; I'm a youngling now,
I've got that dying fall inside my belly.

[32]

Spring's got me, but this season isn't spring.
I feel gymnastic, but this isn't spring.
Am I standing in the rain, what is this water?
Why, there's a flower but it isn't spring,
Nor is it raining; but she's coming back.

(HIPPOLYTA comes back.)

But I love you; look, I thought I was all wet.
Why, I am wet; it's moisture from the trees.
This is silly water that's got onto me;
This is foolish liquid that came down on me.
Why, I'm coming down with a big laughing fit.

HIPPOLYTA
What's the matter with you; am I funny looking?

HERCULES
I get the belly-laughs, and laugh and laugh
At nothing or myself; I just burst out
Laughing and roaring, making the land echo.
Others go mad and drag down oaken trees
Or pull mares through the dirt; but I do this
In a laughing fit.

HIPPOLYTA
But what are you laughing for?

HERCULES
I'm not yet started; I love you, my dear.
Indeed I do in spite of big, loud laughter,
And riotous; I love you like myself.
No, better than myself; I do adore you.
Don't mistrust me, sir or miss; I love you much.
I'll stay with you and always be your husband.
You will be queen of me.

HIPPOLYTA
> But this is sudden.

HERCULES
Oh, everything is very sudden with me.
My food is sudden, love is; sleep is sudden.

HIPPOLYTA
I believe you love me.

HERCULES
> Can you doubt it, dear.
It came on sudden in the midst of dreams.
A dream awakens love: now I'm no more
The hero, but a little boy of sorts;
Caress me, throw me down, and strike me hard.
Here, step upon my foot as I did yours;
Put me in a pen and lock me up somewhere;
Make me do duties: have you stables to clean,
Orchards to gather?

HIPPOLYTA
> My dear, my dearest dear.
You shall stay near me; you're a little boy,
You're a child, a little mischief-man; but no—
You're vast, and I adore you; make me a swing
In this tree and swing me; no, I'll hold your hand.

HERCULES
You've done all that; but I will do the work.
Ah, loved one, but a kiss, another kiss,
As I sling the rope and make a swing for you.
There up, my love; see, I'm your negro slave;
I was black once, but now I'm white, all white
For weakness.

HIPPOLYTA
               Why, you overpower me
With weakness.

               HERCULES
               Shall I build the queen a fire
Or put one out for her?

               HIPPOLYTA
               Well, let me see.

               HERCULES
Say anything: you said you'd run away
With me, and leave your crown here in the bushes;
Let's do it.

               HIPPOLYTA
               No, it's pleasant in this place;
Let's swing.

               HERCULES
               I beg you make me do something.
Can't I split tough, old wood, or bring it in;
Can't I chop down a tree, or dig a hole
To bury a horse in; I can work in leather
Though nothing else: would you be wanting a saddle
Or some boots?

               HIPPOLYTA
               I thought you couldn't do anything.

               HERCULES
I can't; to hell with all the artistry—
My artistry is force: I sculpture strife
And paint the battlefield; once labor done,
I indulge myself, but now I would do chores.

HIPPOLYTA
You tempt me, dear; you know that women take
Advantage of such offers.

HERCULES
Well I know it.

HIPPOLYTA
Do homage to me then, bow down the knee,
Put forehead to the earth, lay belly on loam,
Turn, twine with ecstasy of adoration,
Roll like the dog, the horse: be animal
With rapture.

HERCULES
Sure as life itself, my queen;
I'll do the pony tricks, the tricks of dogs;
I'll roll, and give the paw, and lick the lovely.
I'll tootle my tongue, I'll lisp with all the waters
Of my mouth; see, see, no beaten slave or beast
Was ever lower; see me snake it humble.

HIPPOLYTA
You go too far.

HERCULES
No, never far enough.
I want to go much further; walk on me.
Don't be too careful—walk my rug of brawn
But don't slip on it.

HIPPOLYTA
I'll do it for fun;
Oh, I wish the girls were here to see this scene.

HERCULES
Then, sweetheart, call them in and let them see it.
No reason this should be unknown, unseen.

HIPPOLYTA
Then I shall call them. Girls, girls, come here quick.
      (They come in with ANTIOPE*)*
See, Hercules adores me.

ALL
  Who'd believe it?

HERCULES
I submit to her; I've found a master at last.
I'll live here now: be the queen's hunting dog,
Her nigger, her tame Arab, luscious bull-man.
I'll be her chambermaid, her kitchen girl,
Her turnspit, lickspit.

HIPPOLYTA
  Will you wear the clothes
Of woman as you did for your Omphale?

HERCULES
Give me a dress and a flower for my hair;
This skirt of yours that hangs upon a bush—
See it upon me.

ALL
  It becomes you, girl.

HERCULES
See me, girls. Come round and kiss me, girls.
Now no rough ways. Great gods, I'm in a camp.
Don't rape me, please. I went out for a walk
A virgin. No harm done, my good fellows.

[37]

But let me go; I don't sell anything
Nor am I giving anything away.
I am no whore but a girl of honest parents.
My grandfather was rich; don't ever think wrong
Because I went off walking by myself.
Leave off now, sirs.

HIPPOLYTA
                    We'll keep the young girl here.
She shall be useful round about myself.
This handsome bitch shall be taught that men are men
And camps the camps of men; but she shall follow
Our army, and be with us in our tents.

HERCULES
Oh, soldiers, out upon them—roughs and tramps
Are what you are; but lay a hand on me;
For I have brothers, fathers, sweethearts, too,
And they'll all come at you.

HIPPOLYTA
                    Come into my tent,
Fair one.

(She leads HERCULES into the tent and then returns.)
                    What think you of this hero, girls?

ALL
Astonishing to think of power of love.

HIPPOLYTA
For me he puts on woman's clothes and stuff.
I have no doubt that I could conquer him.
Strange, too, that as his adoration turns
To me, my love grows less.

ANTIOPE
>Then strike him down.

HIPPOLYTA
Not that, for I have other thoughts for him.
We'll make some dresses for him; all of you
Contribute; we'll amuse ourselves by painting
His cheeks and lips and doing over his hair.

ANTIOPE
Couldn't you, my beloved majesty,
Put him in a cage and bind him?

HIPPOLYTA
>Perhaps I could.

ALL
Do it then.

HIPPOLYTA
>Perhaps I will, but here he is
Prancing and dancing and swaying with allure.
Upon my soul he is a greatsome heifer,
A cow of the dawn, a big barbarian whore.

>*(Reenter* HERCULES.*)*

HERCULES
O girls, I know a very pretty dance.
Come gather around and foot it; I will show you
How we weak women do it; I will soften
This rude, crude life, and make you kinder men.
You need a woman's care; but just one thing—
You mustn't get to fighting over me—
No never, never, never.

(He dances; they dance, with the Amazons dancing their way out.)

Hippolyta
Your reputation will suffer, my good girl.

Hercules
What do I care, what do I care; for sure
A woman is master of her own desires.

Hippolyta
You must face hardship.

Hercules
Why, I'll wear my hands
Right down to the bone for all you hearty fellows.
They treat me well at home, but oh, my love,
I was brought up to have nice things enough.
I was always given my way; but I leave all
For you and the greenwood.

Hippolyta
That's a splendid girl.
I'll see that you don't get yourself in trouble—
My men will drink.

Hercules
I can defend myself.
Ever since I was a little toddling girl
I've done it; no one can say Hercules
Was careless ever.

Hippolyta
You had better be careful.

Hercules
O men, I know men; I know them well—
Those harum-scarum men.

HIPPOLYTA
Well, so be it.
You know about men.

HERCULES
Why, so do I, my lover.

HIPPOLYTA
Come, be yourself, my love; this playing woman
Will weaken you; whoever takes this part
Runs risk; the strongest of us must beware
Of the woman in them.

HERCULES
You made me a woman;
You asked for this; let me wash dirty clothes
For the soldiers.

HIPPOLYTA
Suit yourself, my little one.

HERCULES
O my dear days as the darling of the phalanx,
The daughter of it; some harsh, rough old sergeant
Will uncle me; my honor will be the password—
The company will be giving me in marriage
To some soldier boy.

HIPPOLYTA
My dear, don't take on so.
I want you to sew buttons, patch my clothes.
You'll be my little laundress; perhaps as such
You'll be a treasure.

[41]

                    HERCULES
                                Oh, I'll be a treasure.
And I will be your pot boy and your bus boy;
I'm in a giving mood.

                    HIPPOLYTA
                                Then let me shame you
Before the girls, tie you up in hard ropes,
And show you bound.

                    HERCULES
                                Go on and tie me up.

                                        (She ties him up.)

                    HIPPOLYTA
You look so quaint.

                    HERCULES
                                Yes, stand and laugh at me,
I who could lift (I do not mean just pilfer)
But raise upon my shoulders men's great oxen
And those of the gods—those gold, immortal beefs—
Among the narrow hills; so see me now
A dried-and-hung-one even in your hands.

                    HIPPOLYTA
Ha, ha, my love, no more you'll foot the country,
Descending toward the evening to the house
Of the farmer; and your swaggering down lanes
Through goat pastures and past the honey hives
Is done for.

                    HERCULES
                                Yes, no more my soft dog-trot
Among the bean-sheaves.

Hippolyta
      No more hay-tossing,
Horse-training now. O girls, girls girls, girls,
Come here and see the mighty hero now.

    (She goes out to get them; enter Antiope.*)*

Antiope
So she has bound you up, you mighty one,
You one of the gold apples, you bear-baiter
And teaser of the bulls, you golden bummer
Of women; let me tell you to beware—
She's out of love with you; she'll do you harm,
And never give you the girdle.

      *(*Hippolyta *brings in the girls.)*

Hippolyta
      See, I told you.
See what I have, the hero tied with ropes.
Girls, look at him, the captive of your queen.
Look at him, stroke him, sit upon his head.
Tickle the mighty bottoms of his feet.
I give him over to you, pimples and all
Ingrowing hairs and warts upon his neck.

All
What prowess of our queen—this man brought low.
Let's beat him with green sticks, let's roll him over,
Write on him with charcoal, make his fingers crack
And put a long goose feather up his nose.
Let's prod his neck with a sharp pointed stake,
Tie him with ribbons, marry him with rings.

HERCULES
O girls, go easy with this fallen hero.
What are you—Arabs, Abyssinians,
That you would see my blood; let go, let go—
Hounds, beagles—ouch.

HIPPOLYTA
No, gently play with him.
Roll him over, use him to crush scorpions,
And then put the crushed insect on his wound.

HERCULES
Oh, please, Oh, please, Oh, please; but you can't hurt me.

ALL
Oh, can't we, sir; here, pluck us branches green—
We will lay on.

(They beat him.)

HERCULES
The gods, but women are cruel.
There's nothing soft about you soldier-sluts.
You strike like blacksmiths, negroes of the forge.
You cure my hide.

HIPPOLYTA
Girls, you have done enough.

HERCULES
You hurt me, yes, you do, you massacre me.
You kill me off, you do; you ruin me.

HIPPOLYTA
Come, come, with but one shrug you could break loose.

[44]

HERCULES
No, I couldn't either; really I could not.
I'm in your power, queen.

HIPPOLYTA
You let me bind you.

HERCULES
I didn't either; why, I fought with you.

HIPPOLYTA
You are so meek we'd better take advantage.
Girls, whip him up, so you can tell the world
How Hercules was beaten, made all rosy
With sticks and stones.

HERCULES
Sure, ladies, take your fill.

ANTIOPE
Strike him again. O queen, all hail to you.
Don't let him go; he is your golden trophy.
No other woman has secured this man
As you have; kill him.

HIPPOLYTA
No, I won't do that.
But I may keep him tied a little while,
And take new liberties; come here, you girls,
And bring me that basket of old rotten eggs.

GIRL
Here are your eggs.

HIPPOLYTA
Look, little Hercules,
Here are some eggs.

[45]

(She turns a basket of eggs on his head; HERCULES *jumps up, throwing off the ropes.)*

HERCULES

By the gods, who did that?
A joke's a joke but there's an end to it.
I'd rather there were gore upon my face
Than these rotten yolks.

(He takes HIPPOLYTA *by the throat.)*

HIPPOLYTA

Peace with you, Hercules.

HERCULES

By the gods I know not whether to destroy you
Or kiss you.

HIPPOLYTA

Eggs will be good for your hair.

HERCULES

By heavens you lead me to the nearest horse-trough.
I'll make you wash my head, clean out my ears.
You shall make my neck shine.

HIPPOLYTA

I will groom you, lad.

(She leads him to the brook.)

ANTIOPE

Now watch it, women; he may do her harm.
Stand close, and if he makes a move at her,
Run forward.

           ALL
               Yes, we're keeping our eyes open.

           ANTIOPE
I know she will resist him; when you see her
Defend herself, rush out and set your spears
Against him.

           ALL
               We'll watch and keep us ready.

       (HERCULES *and* HIPPOLYTA *return from the brook.*)

           HERCULES
Now you've got me clean again, enough, my love.
I'll leave upon my journey; give me up.
You love me now no longer; the ambition
Of a soldier has got back into your heart.
I see it, and I make myself absurd
By this masquerade. You loved me at the start
But now that I love you, your love is over.
The queen has gotten back into your body;
You think how you can make use of my love,
Putting me to more tasks.

           HIPPOLYTA
               You don't love me,
If you think so.

           HERCULES
               Though I am Hercules
And in love, I still can think.

           HIPPOLYTA
               That is good.
           [47]

HERCULES
No, I must have your girdle and depart.
You're wholly out of love.

HIPPOLYTA
No, my darling one,
Don't go. I love to be a hostess to you;
Never did we have such dear jockey with us
Before—such a ruddy tamer of the lions,
Such a cowherd, such a rustler and a hustler
Of men and oxen, such a death on foxes,
Such a turner-inside-out of dogs and horses
As you; it's pleasure to have a big Bumps
And Bruises like yourself to hog our victuals
And lick our platters.

HERCULES
At your service, sir.

HIPPOLYTA
Come, dear, and let us be political.
You said I had a face to keep up here
And so indeed I have; it's about my girdle—
I even tried to force the belt on you
But a little while ago; but now I must
Do otherwise.

HERCULES
Dear, I must have the girdle.

HIPPOLYTA
I know you must; and you can have it, dear.
You said yourself that we should act a part,
And you should tear it from me, while I acted
To keep it.

[48]

HERCULES

I will tear it off from you
And give you a few bats upon the legs
With it. Come, give me up that girdle
Or I'll cut you one.

HIPPOLYTA

I'll never give the girdle.

HERCULES

Come, give it to me, give it to me, I say.
No fooling, fighting. Give me up the girdle.

(They pretend to struggle. The Amazons attack in earnest.)

Get away, you women. Get yourself out of here.
Get out, get out.

HIPPOLYTA

They only just pretend.

HERCULES

They do not so.

HIPPOLYTA

Please hold your anger, dear.

HERCULES

But by my body but this is a grind
Of flesh, the slap, the punch. How goes it, queen?
I'll pound and pummel.

(He fights the Amazons off.)

HIPPOLYTA

Stop. Don't hurt the girls.
They've had enough. You've given it them hard.

HERCULES
And I'll give you one blow for fun of it.

(He strikes her.)

HIPPOLYTA
Oh, that one hurt. I think I'm killed by it.

(She falls and dies.)

ALL
O heavens, is she hurt?

HERCULES
It's just a joke.
She couldn't be hurt that much.

ANTIOPE
The queen is dead.

HERCULES
She isn't dead. Why, I just lightly touched her.
That blow would never have harmed a three-years child.
She's fooling, feigning fainting. Pick her up.
No, I will pick her up.

ALL
She's dead, she's dead.

(He looks close at her.)

HERCULES
By heavens, you are right, and I have killed her.
Hippolyta, poor woman of the woods,
Queen of the deer as well as warrior-girls—
I've laid you out.

ALL

>Yes, you have killed the queen.

HERCULES

By heavens, I'm sorry. But an hour ago
I loved her, but there's no use crying for it.
She's dead and I am sorry: that is all,
And you and I must make the best of it.
But you, Antiope, you shall not reign
In her place. Die too, and lie there; let her lie,

>*(He kills* ANTIOPE.*)*

But bury the queen in the best way you can.
I'll out of here; but heavens, I forgot
The girdle; give it to me.

>*(He takes the girdle from* HIPPOLYTA.*)*
>With this gold strap

I do another deed. Goodbye, you women.
Don't cry too long, but get another queen.
Goodbye, wild ones, goodbye, and think of me
In the green pastures and the starry plains,
Goodbye, goodbye.

>*(He leaves. The women bend over* HIPPOLYTA.*)*